ANN ROSSI

FREEDOM STRUGGLE

The Anti-Slavery Movement in America
1830–1865

NATIONAL GEOGRAPHIC

Washington, D.C.

Cover Bettmann/CORBIS; pp. 1, 2–7 (border); 3 (2nd from left), 4, 12, 19 (right), 21–13 (border), 26–27 (border), 32, 36, 40 CORBIS; pp. 1 (left & right), 3 (right), 7, 9, 11, 14, 15, 17, 19 (bot.), 21 (top), 22, 23, 25 (top), 26, 28, 29 (border), 30 (right), 32–33 (border), 35 (top), 37 Bettmann/CORBIS; pp. 3 (left & 2nd from right), 8 National Portrait Gallery, Smithsonian Institution/Art Resource; pp. 2, 24 (bot.), 30–31 (bkgd.), 31 (bot.) Historical Picture Archive/CORBIS; p. 5 Snark/Art Resource, NY; pp. 6, 25 (bot.) Scala/Art Resource, NY; pp. 9–13 (border), 15–19 (border), 35–40 (border) Skycraft Marble Desi/CORBIS; p. 10 (left & right) Massachusetts Historical Society; pp. 13, 16 Bridgeman Art Library; p. 19 (mid.) AP Photo Archive; p. 19 (top) Collins Art; p. 20 North Wind Picture Archives; p. 21 (bot.) Library of Congress; p. 24 (top) William H.Seward House; p. 27 Francis G. Mayer/CORBIS; p. 29 (top) The Granger Collection, NY; p. 29 (bot.) South Carolina State Museum; pp. 30 (left), 35 (bot.) Chicago Historical Society; p. 31 (top) Réunion du Musées Nationaux/Art Resource, NY; pp. 33, 34 The Pennsylvania Academy for Fine Arts; p. 38 Smithsonian Museum of American Art/Art Resource, NY.

Library of Congress Cataloging-in-Publication Data
Rossi, Ann.
   Freedom struggle : the anti-slavery movement, 1830–1865 / by Ann Rossi.
      v. cm. — (Crossroads America)
      ISBN: 0-7922-7828-3   Includes index.
Contents: Slavery, right or wrong?—The Underground Railroad—Slavery divides the nation—Points of view, should slavery be abolished?—The Path to War—Primary sources, Uncle Tom's Cabin—Fighting for freedom. 35 1. Antislavery movements—United States—History—19th century—Juvenile literature. 2. Abolitionists—United States—History—19th century—Juvenile literature. 3. Underground railroad—Juvenile literature. 4. Slavery—United States—History—Juvenile literature. 5. Slaves—Emancipation—United States—Juvenile literature. 6. African Americans—History—To 1863—Juvenile literature. [1. Antislavery movements. 2. Underground railroad. 3. Slavery—History. 5. African Americans—History—To 1863.] I. Title. II. Series.
E449 .R83 2005
973.7'114—dc22
                    2003019824

Produced through the worldwide resources of the National Geographic Society, John M. Fahey, Jr., President and Chief Executive Officer; Gilbert M. Grosvenor, Chairman of the Board; Nina D. Hoffman, Executive Vice President and President, Books and Education Publishing; Ericka Markman, President, Children's Books and Education Publishing Group; Nancy Feresten, Vice President, Children's Books, Editor-in-Chief; Steve Mico, Vice President Education Publishing Group, Editorial Director; Marianne Hiland, Editorial Manager; Anita Schwartz, Project Editor; Tara Peterson, Editorial Assistant; Jim Hiscott, Design Manager; Linda McKnight, Art Director; Diana Bourdrez, Anne Whittle, Photo Research; Matt Wascavage, Manager of Publishing Services; Sean Philpotts, Production Coordinator; Jane Ponton, Production Artist; Susan Donnelly, Children's Books Project Editor. Production: Clifton M. Brown III, Manufacturing and Quality Control.

PROGRAM DEVELOPMENT
Gare Thompson Associates, Inc.

CONSULTANTS/REVIEWERS
Dr. Russell Adams, Afro-American Studies Dept., Howard University, Washington, D.C.;
Dr. Margit E. McGuire, School of Education, Seattle University, Seattle, Washington

BOOK DESIGN
Steven Curtis Design, Inc.

NATIONAL GEOGRAPHIC SOCIETY
1145 17th Street, N.W.
Washington, D.C. 20036-4688

Printed in Mexico

Table of Contents

Frederick Douglass Harriet Tubman John Brown Harriet Beecher Stowe

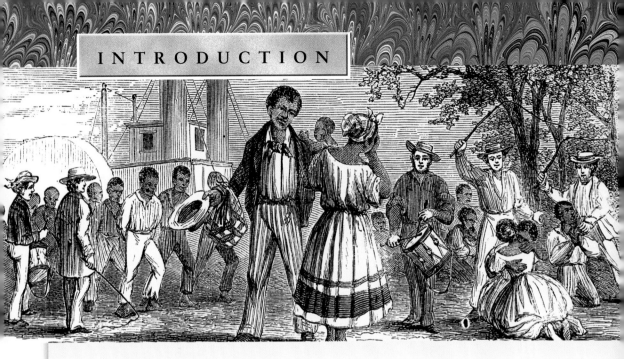

America in 1860

THE ROOTS OF SLAVERY

*I*n 1860, nearly 4 million black people were slaves in the United States.* Slavery in America was far older than the United States itself. Africans were first brought as laborers to the English colony of Virginia in 1619. By the 1660's, most Africans in the colony had been made slaves. Some American colonists, especially in the South, needed many workers to grow crops such as tobacco, rice, and cotton.

At first, most of these workers were **indentured servants** from Europe. In exchange for the cost of their trip to America, they worked for a master for a fixed number of years. Then they were freed. Indentured servants worked hard. Many masters treated their servants cruelly. After 1680, fewer indentured servants came to America. So slave traders brought more Africans here.

In 1680, blacks made up less than 7 percent of Virginia's population. By 1750, they were nearly 44 percent.

Unlike indentured servants, enslaved Africans came to America against their will. They were torn from everything they knew—family, home, and culture. They were bought and sold. Slave owners saw slaves not as human beings but as property. Children whose mothers were slaves became slaves too. Slaves could not leave their owner's land without a written pass. They were often punished.

By 1808, it was against U.S. law to import more slaves. At that time, there were about one million slaves in the United States. Since no more slaves were being imported, the value of those already here increased greatly. The slave trade in the United States became a big business. But some Americans thought slavery was wrong. They struggled to abolish, or end, slavery. Because of this, they were called **abolitionists**.

LIFE UNDER SLAVERY

Most slaves worked in the fields. They plowed, planted, and harvested crops. On smaller farms, slaves often worked beside their owners. But on larger farms called plantations, an overseer or slave driver supervised the slaves. If slaves made a mistake or didn't work quickly enough, the overseer might beat them.

Owners could treat their slaves almost any way they wished. They could sell or trade their slaves anytime. Slave families were often broken up. Mothers, fathers, and children might be sold to different owners.

Slave owners decided what their slaves did and how many hours they worked. Most slaves worked all year, in all kinds of weather. During harvest season, slaves would begin work before sunrise and continue into the night.

MISSISSIPPI COTTON PLANTATION

Slave children usually started working when they were eight years old. Some started sooner. They would do the easier chores. They pulled weeds, fetched water, and gathered wood. On cotton plantations, most house servants were children. The men and women were needed to work in the fields. A slave was considered an adult by age twelve.

Owners gave their slaves food, clothing, and housing. But they didn't pay them. Many slaves lived in windowless, one-room cabins with dirt floors. They were often hungry and cold in winter. Many slaves raised food in small gardens they tended after their long workday had ended.

IN THEIR OWN WORDS

"As a young child I had no bed. I must have perished with the cold, but that, the coldest nights, I used to steal a bag which was used for carrying corn to the mill. I would crawl into this bag, and there sleep on the cold, damp, clay floor."

Frederick Douglass

"I am not only an American slave, but a man, and as such, am bound to use my powers for the welfare of the whole human brotherhood."

Frederick Douglass

CHAPTER 1

Slavery: Right or Wrong?

SLAVE AUCTION

FREDERICK DOUGLASS

In 1838, a young black man escaped from what he later called "the dark night of slavery" in Maryland. In the North, he joined the anti-slavery movement, and became a powerful speaker and writer. The young man worked hard to end slavery and fought for equality for all people. His name was Frederick Douglass.

Douglass was born a slave around 1818. One of his owners started to teach eight-year-old Frederick to read. But this was against the law. So her husband made her stop. Southerners feared that teaching slaves to read would make them unfit to be slaves. Frederick understood that being able to read was a path to freedom. He decided to learn to read anyway. And he did!

Frederick had many different masters. Some were cruel. Frederick saw many slaves being whipped. He was beaten too. But Frederick fought back. He promised himself he would be free one day.

After his escape, Douglass worried that slave catchers might find him. So he went to Europe to be safe. He spent nearly two years there. He made many speeches against slavery. During that time, abolitionist friends bought Douglass's freedom from his owners. Overjoyed, he came back to America. Douglass kept fighting against slavery. His work made him famous. He made many people realize that America could not be a free country while slavery existed there.

THE ABOLITIONISTS ORGANIZE

The anti-slavery movement drew blacks and whites, Northerners and Southerners, rich and poor, men and women. Among the movement's leaders were William Lloyd Garrison and Wendell Phillips, two white men from Massachusetts. They were joined in the American Anti-Slavery Society by the daughters of a South Carolina slave owner, Sarah and Angelina Grimké. The Grimké sisters had seen slavery up-close as children. In the 1830s, their accounts of its horrors attracted large audiences in the North.

Abolitionists used accounts of slavery by former slaves, such as Frederick Douglass, to turn people against it. For years, supporters of slavery had claimed that slaves lived a happy life. They said that masters gave their slaves good homes. But former slaves told another story.

Douglass told how slave children were treated like animals. They were called to eat cornmeal mush from a trough. As a child, Douglass fought the dogs for scraps of food. Meanwhile, slave owners feasted on fine foods. Douglass described how he and other slaves were cruelly beaten. Horrified by the stories, many people became abolitionists.

SARAH (LEFT) AND ANGELINA GRIMKÉ

"I have seen slavery. I know it has horrors that can never be described. I was brought up under its wing. I saw for many years how it destroys human happiness."

Angelina Grimké

FREDERICK DOUGLASS SPEAKING AT AN ANTI-SLAVERY MEETING

SLAVES PICKING COTTON

SLAVERY AND MONEY

One way the abolitionists tried to fight slavery was to boycott, or refuse to buy, products made by slaves. Abolitionists hoped that slave owners would free their slaves if they could not sell slave-made goods. But the boycotts didn't work because few people joined them. The problem was that too many Americans were making money from slavery.

The Southern economy was based on slavery. Farming was the main business in the South. Landowners needed their slaves to plant and harvest their crops. Southerners feared their economy would fail without slaves.

Cotton was an ideal crop for the growing conditions in the South. But a worker needed an entire day to clean a single pound of cotton by hand. Then in 1793, Eli Whitney invented the cotton gin. This machine could clean more than 50 pounds of cotton in a day. Southern dependence on slavery increased as more and more Southerners began to raise cotton.

Cotton mills in England and in the Northern states bought as much cotton as the South could produce. Plantation owners needed more slaves to work in the cotton fields. As the demand for slaves increased, prices for good workers increased too. Trading in slaves became very profitable.

Even though industry in the North did not use slaves, many people there did not agree with the abolitionists. Thousands of Northerners depended on slave-grown cotton for their living.

STEAMBOATS WAITING TO LOAD COTTON AT NEW ORLEANS

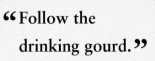
"Follow the drinking gourd."

Refrain of a slave song telling runaways to use the group of stars called the "drinking gourd" (or Big Dipper) to guide them north

PEOPLE HELPING RUNAWAY SLAVES AT A STATION ON THE UNDERGROUND RAILROAD IN INDIANA.

CHAPTER 2

The Underground Railroad

ABOLITIONISTS IN PHILADELPHIA HELPING HENRY "BOX" BROWN OUT OF HIS CRATE

THE WAY TO FREEDOM

Like Frederick Douglass, many slaves ran away from their owners. Slaves headed for free states in the North, or Canada. They traveled at night and followed the North Star to freedom. Some used clever tricks to escape. One man, Henry Brown, got inside a wooden crate and had himself shipped to Philadelphia.

Abolitionists, including free black people, helped many slaves reach safety. The **"Underground Railroad"** became the name for the network of people who helped runaway slaves escape. One story says the name was first used in 1831. A slave being chased by his master crossed the Ohio River. Then he disappeared as if he had "gone off on an underground road."

The people who ran the Underground Railroad used railroading terms as code words. *Stations* were hiding places where fugitives could rest and eat. The homes of Frederick Douglass and thousands of other abolitionists were stations.

Conductors were people who guided runaways, or *passengers,* from one station to another. Often they walked. But they also used whatever means of transportation they could find.

Running away was dangerous. Runaways didn't always know whom they could trust. If they were captured, they were punished severely. And people who helped runaways were punished too.

FIGHTING THE SLAVE CATCHERS

Some slaves risked their lives to help other slaves escape. For four years, Arnold Gragston rowed slaves from Kentucky across the Ohio River. On the other side of the river was Ohio, a free state. He made the trip on moonless nights. In the daytime, Gragston was back at work on the plantation.

One time he was nearly caught after ferrying 12 people to freedom. So Gragston made one last trip. He rowed himself and his wife across the river. But they didn't dare stay in Ohio. They were afraid of slave catchers. Instead, they made their way farther north to Detroit, Michigan.

RUNAWAY SLAVES FLEEING NORTH TO FREEDOM

John Price was another slave who escaped to Ohio. He decided to settle in the peaceful college town of Oberlin, Ohio. He lived and worked there for more than two years. Then in 1858, Anderson Jennings, a slave catcher from Kentucky, arrived in town. He would get a $500 reward if he captured John Price.

Jennings nearly got the reward. He and two partners captured Price. But Price saw a student he knew and yelled for aid. The student raced to Oberlin to get help. Jennings and his partners had taken Price to a hotel to wait for the train. They were stunned when a large crowd surrounded the hotel and demanded that John Price be let go. Then some of the crowd ran into the hotel and rescued Price. They hid him and then took him to Canada.

The U.S. government jailed 37 men who helped Price escape. The government showed that it would punish anyone who helped escaped slaves. But this event also created more anti-slavery feelings in the North.

A SLAVE CATCHER DRAGGING A RUNAWAY BACK TO SLAVERY

IN THEIR OWN WORDS

"The little ones never get tired of hearin' how their grandpa brought freedom to loads of slaves he could touch and feel, but never could see."

Arnold Gragston, describing rowing runaway slaves across the Ohio River at night

HARRIET TUBMAN

Harriet Tubman was one of the most famous conductors on the Underground Railroad. She was born a slave in Maryland around 1820. Even as a young girl, Harriet was brave and liked to help others. As a teenager, she stood between a field slave and an angry overseer. The overseer threw a heavy object at the slave but hit Harriet on the head instead. After that, she suffered from blackouts throughout her life.

In 1849, Tubman thought her owner was planning to sell her. So she ran away. Tubman traveled at night, following the North Star. Friendly people helped her. She reached the North, found a job, and saved her money. But now, Tubman had a bigger goal. She was going to return to the South and help her family to freedom.

The **Fugitive Slave Act** of 1850 made her plan very dangerous. This law said that Americans must not help runaway slaves. But Tubman made it back to Maryland. She brought her sister and her sister's children north to freedom.

Tubman didn't stop going south. She had many more people to free! By 1856, a reward of $40,000 (equal to $800,000 today) was offered for Tubman's capture. She used all kinds of clever tricks to disguise herself. One time she heard slave catchers reading a description of her on a wanted poster. The description said that she couldn't read. So Tubman picked up a book and pretended to read it. In the end, she made a total of 19 trips and rescued about 300 people, including her elderly parents.

IN THEIR OWN WORDS

"There's two things I've got a right to and these are death or liberty. One or the other I mean to have. No one will take me back alive! I shall fight for my liberty!"

Harriet Tubman

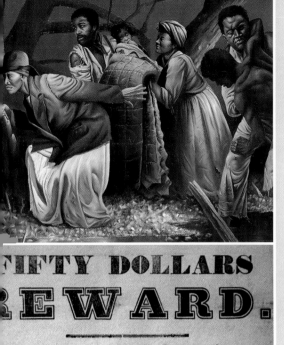

HARRIET TUBMAN (WITH RIFLE) LEADING A BAND OF RUNAWAY SLAVES

HARRIET TUBMAN

REWARD POSTER FOR A RUNAWAY SLAVE

TUBMAN (AT THE LEFT) WITH A GROUP OF FORMER SLAVES SHE RESCUED

FIFTY DOLLARS
REWARD.

an away from Mount Welby, Prince
rge's County, Maryland, on Monday,
2d inst., a negro man calling himself
Bond, about 25 years of age, about
et 6 inches in height, stout built, cop=
complexion; the only mark recol=
ed is a peculiar speck in one of his
. Had on when he went away a frock
ed coat, dark brown, and cap near the
color. I will give twenty-five dollars

"I know no South, no North no East, no West, to which I owe any allegiance. The Union is my country."

Henry Clay

SENATOR HENRY CLAY (STANDING AT THE CENTER) SPEAKING DURING THE DEBATE OVER THE COMPROMISE OF 1850

CHAPTER 3

Slavery Divides the Nation

MOB ATTACKING
ABOLITIONIST WILLIAM
LLOYD GARRISON
(LOWER RIGHT)

FIGHTS OVER NEW STATES

In 1819, the United States was made up of an equal number of free states and slave states. Then Missouri applied for admission to the Union. Slavery was legal in Missouri. Suddenly the balance of power was at risk. Congress worked out a compromise. Missouri was admitted as a slave state, and the northern part of Massachusetts became the free state of Maine. But the **Missouri Compromise** of 1820 was only a temporary solution. The struggle for power between slave states and free states would go on.

By 1850, the issue of slavery threatened to destroy the Union. Congress again found a way to partly satisfy both North and South.

In the **Compromise of 1850,** California was admitted to the Union as a free state. And the slave trade, although not slavery itself, was ended in the District of Columbia. But to satisfy the South, the Fugitive Slave Act of 1850 was passed. It fined or imprisoned people who helped slaves escape. Blacks and many Northerners thought the new Fugitive Slave Act was too harsh. Anger over the new law helped the growth of the anti-slavery movement.

A MAP FROM 1856 SHOWING THE
UNITED STATES DIVIDED INTO FREE
STATES (RED), SLAVE STATES (BROWN),
AND WESTERN TERRITORIES (GREEN)

"A HIGHER LAW"

WILLIAM H. SEWARD

One of those who opposed the Compromise of 1850 was New York Senator William H. Seward. Seward thought that U.S. law should not protect slavery.

Seward was born in 1801 in New York. After college, he became a lawyer. In 1824, Seward married Frances Miller. He soon began a career in politics. Seward was New York's governor from 1839 to 1842. While he was governor, New York passed several anti-slavery laws.

Some laws stopped state officials from capturing escaped slaves. In 1849, Seward was elected to the U.S. Senate. He became one of its most powerful members. In 1850, Seward wanted California admitted as a free state without conditions. He strongly opposed the Fugitive Slave Act.

Seward was a leader of the anti-slavery movement. He and his wife became friends of Harriet Tubman. She used the Sewards' home as an Underground Railroad station. In 1856, Seward helped organize the new Republican Party, which opposed allowing slavery in new territories.

IN THEIR OWN WORDS

"There is a higher law than the Constitution."

William H. Seward

THE "CAST-IRON MAN"

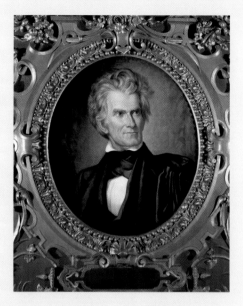

JOHN C. CALHOUN

He served as a member of Congress, secretary of war, vice president, senator, and secretary of state. Calhoun worked hard to promote the South's interests, especially slavery. He argued that slavery had civilized Africans.

Calhoun was too ill to give his final speech about the Compromise of 1850. Another senator read it to the Senate on March 4. In his speech, Calhoun stated that the North needed to honor Southern interests. Otherwise, the Southern states would leave the Union. Calhoun died March 31, 1850.

Senator John C. Calhoun was a fierce supporter of slavery. He was so unwilling to compromise that he became known as "the Cast-Iron Man."

Calhoun was born in 1782 in South Carolina. He graduated from college in 1804 and started to practice law. A few years later, Calhoun began a 40-year political career. In 1811, he married a rich widow, his cousin Floride Calhoun, and later bought a large plantation.

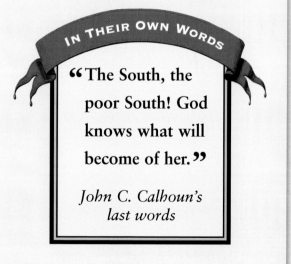

IN THEIR OWN WORDS

"The South, the poor South! God knows what will become of her."

John C. Calhoun's last words

Should Slavery Be Abolished?

William H. Seward and John C. Calhoun had opposite points of view on whether slavery should be abolished.

Seward thought slavery was an evil system causing great harm to the country. He wanted slavery to be abolished. He opposed admitting any new slave states into the Union.

I [agree] in regarding slavery as a great moral evil, as unjust in principle, a violation of human rights and [harmful] to the prosperity and happiness of every people among whom it exists.

SLAVE AUCTION

Our own experience has proved the dangerous influence and tendency of slavery. All our [fears] of dangers, present and future, begin and end with slavery. I cannot consent to introduce slavery into any part of this continent which is now exempt from what seems to me so great an evil.

John C. Calhoun did not want slavery to be abolished. He thought that history showed that slavery was needed for a well-organized society. He believed that without slavery, Southern whites and blacks could not live together in peace.

There never has yet existed a wealthy and civilized society in which one portion of the community did not, in point of fact, live on the labor of the other.

MISSISSIPPI COTTON PLANTATION

Many in the South once believed slavery was a moral and political evil. That folly and delusion are gone. We see it now in its true light and regard it as the most safe and stable basis for free institutions in the world.

We of the South will not, cannot, surrender slavery. To maintain the existing relations between whites and blacks in the South is indispensable to the peace and happiness of both.

Seward and Calhoun had opposite opinions on slavery. But they agreed that this issue would bring the North and South into direct conflict. As Calhoun said, "Abolition and the Union cannot coexist."

"BLEEDING KANSAS"

The Compromise of 1850 didn't end the argument over extending slavery into new states. In 1854, Congress passed the **Kansas-Nebraska Act.** The act created the territories of Kansas and Nebraska. It allowed the people to decide whether their territory would permit slavery. Most Nebraskans opposed slavery. They decided the slavery question quietly. But in Kansas, the pro-slavery and free-state supporters had many battles. As a result, the territory was called "Bleeding Kansas."

Many people flocked to Kansas to help decide the territory's fate. One of them was abolitionist John Brown. He arrived in Kansas in 1855. He brought weapons to his sons who lived there. They feared attacks by pro-slavery forces. Brown had been against slavery since he was a child. One time, Brown stayed with a man who owned a young slave. He never forgot how the man beat his slave.

GUNFIGHT IN A KANSAS TOWN BETWEEN PRO-SLAVERY AND ANTI-SLAVERY FORCES

When he grew up, Brown believed it was his duty to help escaped slaves. He was determined to destroy slavery—by force, if necessary. In May 1856, pro-slavery men burned and looted the anti-slavery town of Lawrence, Kansas. Later that month, Brown led a small band that dragged five pro-slavery men from their homes and killed them. After that, Brown and his followers were wanted for murder. But they avoided capture. In October, Brown left Kansas.

"It's better that 20 bad men should die than that one man who came here to make Kansas a Free State should be driven out."

John Brown

IN THEIR OWN WORDS

"The strife is no longer local, but national."

Charles Sumner

CHAPTER 4

The Path to War

THE CRISIS DEEPENS

DRED SCOTT

The Kansas-Nebraska Act set the nation on a path to civil war. Hatred between pro-slavery and anti-slavery people was growing. Events in Washington, D.C., made things worse. In 1856, Congressman Preston Brooks of South Carolina attacked Charles Sumner, an abolitionist senator from the North. Brooks beat Sumner with a cane until it broke. The attack outraged Northerners. But Brooks' supporters sent him 180 replacement canes.

Many Northerners felt the government was wrong to protect slavery. These feelings grew stronger in 1857 when the Supreme Court ruled on the Dred Scott case. Dred Scott was a slave. His owner took him to Illinois and Wisconsin Territory, where they lived for several years. Slavery was outlawed in both places.

Later, Scott and his owner returned to Missouri, a slave state. After his owner died, anti-slavery supporters filed a lawsuit to win Scott's freedom. His lawyers claimed that Scott was free because he had lived in places where slavery was not allowed.

The Supreme Court ruled that Scott could not bring a lawsuit because blacks were not citizens of the United States. It also said that slavery could not be outlawed in any territory of the United States. The decision outraged abolitionists. They feared that slavery would never be stopped.

TOKENS THAT SLAVES WERE FORCED TO WEAR

Uncle Tom's Cabin

Some of the most powerful arguments against slavery came in a story, *Uncle Tom's Cabin*. It was written by an abolitionist, Harriet Beecher Stowe. The book became an immediate best seller when it was published in 1852. *Uncle Tom's Cabin* convinced many people of the evils of slavery—and brought the Civil War closer. During the war, President Abraham Lincoln met Mrs. Stowe. He greeted her by saying, "So you're the little woman who wrote the book that made this great war!"

BY 1853, *UNCLE TOM'S CABIN* HAD SOLD MORE THAN 300,000 COPIES.

HARRIET BEECHER STOWE

IN THIS SCENE FROM *UNCLE TOM'S CABIN* THE SLAVE ELIZA FLEES FROM SLAVE CATCHERS OVER THE FROZEN OHIO RIVER.

STOWE'S STORY WAS ALSO POPULAR IN EUROPE. THIS FRENCH PLATE SHOWS A SCENE FROM HER BOOK.

L'ONCLE TOM DANS SA CASE

AT THE END OF THE BOOK, THE SAINTLY UNCLE TOM DIES AFTER A BEATING BY THE CRUEL SLAVE DRIVER SIMON LEGREE.

HARPERS FERRY

In the tense atmosphere of the late 1850s, both Northerners and Southerners were frightened. What would happen next? The answer was given by John Brown.

Brown had a bold plan. He wanted to start a slave uprising. Brown raised money and gathered weapons. He found and trained recruits. Brown also met with Harriet Tubman to learn her escape routes from the South. Brown planned to rescue slaves. Then he would lead them to freedom in Canada. Brown planned to start his rescue by capturing the town of Harpers Ferry, Virginia. A government arsenal—a storehouse for weapons—was there. He wanted Frederick Douglass to join him. But Douglass tried to convince him that the plan would fail.

One night in October 1859, Brown and his men captured the arsenal, other buildings, and two bridges in Harpers Ferry. Then some of his men went to nearby plantations to capture slave owners. Several slaves joined Brown's men. So far, no blood had been shed.

But then Brown's men stopped a train and shot a man. Chaos followed. Church bells rang. People yelled that a slave uprising was taking place. Local troops arrived, and fighting began. Brown took shelter with some of his men and their prisoners in an engine house.

TROOPS ATTACKING BROWN AND HIS MEN AT HARPERS FERRY

U.S. troops arrived. Brown refused to surrender. The soldiers stormed the engine house. Brown was wounded and captured. He was quickly tried and convicted. In early December, Brown was hanged. His raid on Harpers Ferry further divided the nation. The attack panicked many Southerners. They thought the raid was part of a Northern plot to end slavery by force. But many Northerners thought Brown was a hero.

"John Brown's zeal in the cause of my race was far greater than mine. I could live for the slave, but he could die for him."

Frederick Douglass

JOHN BROWN BEING TAKEN TO BE HANGED

"I wish we had a hundred thousand colored troops. We would put an end to this war."

Frederick Douglass's son, Lewis, sergeant major in the 54th Massachusetts

THE 54TH MASSACHUSETTS, FIRST AFRICAN-AMERICAN TROOPS TO SERVE IN THE UNION ARMY

Fighting for Freedom

EMANCIPATION
PROCLAMATION
BEING READ TO SLAVES

THE WAR COMES

In 1860, Abraham Lincoln became president. Although he had always hated slavery, Lincoln was not an abolitionist. But to Southerners, his election was a bad sign. They feared the government would no longer protect their interests. Before Lincoln was sworn in on March 4, 1861, South Carolina, Mississippi, Florida, Alabama, Georgia, Louisiana, and Texas left the Union. They formed the **Confederate States of America**. Virginia, Arkansas, Tennessee, and North Carolina joined the other Southern states later. In April 1861, the Civil War broke out.

Frederick Douglass and other abolitionists tried to persuade Lincoln to emancipate, or free, the slaves. They argued the South was using slaves to help their war effort. If slaves were freed, the South would lose workers. And freed slaves would fight for the North.

Finally, on January 1, 1863, Lincoln issued the **Emancipation Proclamation**. It freed all slaves in the parts of the Confederate states that were in rebellion. It also allowed for the recruiting of black soldiers. By the end of the war in 1865, more than 200,000 African-American men had fought for the Union. One in five died.

Black soldiers had to overcome the prejudice of most white army officers. Their bravery in battle changed many minds. As Frederick Douglass said, once a black man had served in the army "no power on earth can deny that he has earned the right to citizenship."

AFRICAN-AMERICAN
SOLDIER

35

STRUGGLING FOR EQUALITY

The Civil War ended in April 1865. The South was part of the United States again. But abolitionists still had work to do. They wanted the Constitution to end slavery. So they organized a campaign for an amendment, or change, to the Constitution. The **Thirteenth Amendment** became law in December 1865. It abolished slavery. After more than 200 years, all African Americans were free at last!

These freed slaves faced many problems. The war had left many Southerners—both former slaves and poor whites—hungry and homeless. To help them, the government set up the **Freedmen's Bureau**. The Bureau gave needy Southerners food and clothing. It trained teachers, set up schools, gave job training, and helped people find work. The Freedmen's Bureau also ran hospitals.

Frederick Douglass and other abolitionists worked hard to get legal rights for free blacks. In 1868, the **Fourteenth Amendment** gave citizenship to former slaves. It guaranteed their freedom and right to be treated fairly and equally. It also gave male African Americans aged 21 and older the right to vote. Then in 1870, the **Fifteenth Amendment** said that citizens could not lose the right to vote because of their race, color, or prior status as a slave. But there was still much to be done.

FORMER SLAVES LEARNING TO READ IN A FREEDMEN'S BUREAU SCHOOL

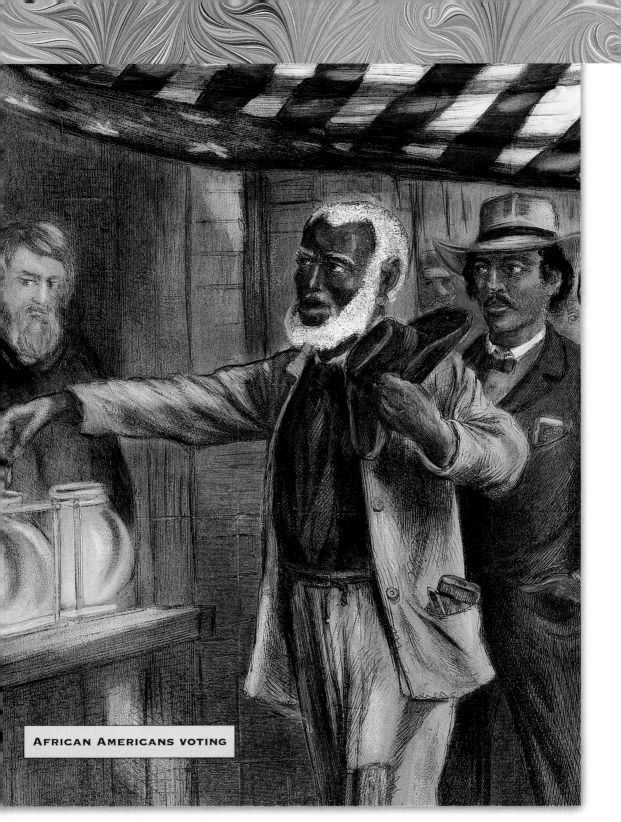

AFRICAN AMERICANS VOTING

Legacy

After the Civil War, white Southerners tried to keep control of the economy and government of the South. They tried to limit where and how African Americans worked. They did not want African Americans to vote. Some whites used terrorism to keep blacks from voting. Many African Americans were beaten or even killed.

Until he died in 1895, Frederick Douglass continued to fight for equal rights. But it would take many years of struggle to gain equality for African Americans. Real change did not come until the Civil Rights Movement of the 1950s and 1960s. The example of abolitionists like Frederick Douglass and Harriet Tubman continues to inspire those who work for freedom and justice in American society.

Glossary

ABOLITIONIST a person who wanted to abolish, or end, slavery

COMPROMISE OF 1850 series of laws that admitted California as a free state, left the question of slavery in the new territories of the West to be decided by their people, and promised a stronger law to help slave owners recapture runaway slaves

CONFEDERATE STATES OF AMERICA confederation formed in 1861 by 11 Southern states after they left the United States

EMANCIPATION PROCLAMATION 1863 order by U.S. President Abraham Lincoln that freed all slaves in the parts of the Confederate states that were in rebellion

FIFTEENTH AMENDMENT change to the U.S. Constitution, passed in 1870, that protected African-American voting rights

FOURTEENTH AMENDMENT change to the U.S. Constitution, passed in 1868, that made former slaves citizens

FREEDMEN'S BUREAU federal agency set up to help former slaves after the Civil War

FUGITIVE SLAVE ACT 1850 law that encouraged the capture of runaway slaves by punishing people who helped them

INDENTURED SERVANT a person who worked for a master in the American colonies for a fixed number of years in exchange for the cost of the trip there

KANSAS-NEBRASKA ACT 1854 law creating the territories of Kansas and Nebraska and allowing their people to decide whether to permit slavery

MISSOURI COMPROMISE series of laws passed in 1820 to keep the balance between slave states and free states in the Union

THIRTEENTH AMENDMENT change to the U.S. Constitution, passed in 1865, that outlawed slavery

UNDERGROUND RAILROAD network of people who helped runaway slaves escape

Index